FACTS AND FICTION ABOUT DRUGS™

I0800022

HEROIN

PHILIP WOLNY

rosen publishing's
rosen central
New York

Published in 2020 by The Rosen Publishing Group, Inc.
29 East 21st Street, New York, NY 10010

First Edition

Cataloging-in-Publication Data

Names: Wolny, Philip, author.
Title: Heroin / Philip Wolny.
Description: First Edition. | New York : Rosen Publishing, 2020 | Series: Facts and fiction about drugs | Includes bibliographical references and index. | Audience: Grades 5–8.
Identifiers: ISBN 9781725347618 (library binding) | ISBN 9781725347601 (paperback)
Subjects: LCSH: Heroin—Juvenile literature. | Heroin abuse—Juvenile literature. | Substance abuse—Juvenile literature.
Classification: LCC HV5822.H4 W65 2020 | DDC 362.29'3—dc23

Some of the images in this book illustrate individuals who are models. The depictions do not imply actual situations or events.

Manufactured in the United States of America

CONTENTS

INTRODUCTION

In Camden, New Jersey, a sickness hit in the 2000s. It hit Camden like it hit so many other places. Family members stole money from one another. Burglaries and robberies rose. More people were going to hospital emergency rooms. People began to die. Welcome to the heroin epidemic, happening in Anytown, USA.

In February 2018, southern New Jersey's *Courier-Post* talked about how heroin had affected Camden, New Jersey. Bill Moen and Josh Moen were brothers who had grown up athletic and happy in town. Josh liked skateboarding and BMX riding, and he would occasionally come home with minor injuries.

In fifth grade, Josh was injured on his bike, and he got his tonsils taken out in the hospital. By year's end, Josh had been prescribed opioids (Percocet and codeine) three times. Because he had taken the drugs legally before, when Josh started taking opioids at high school parties, it didn't seem so bad. "I got hurt quite often," he told the *Courier-Post*. "And taking pills for it never seemed like a big deal to me." The straightlaced athlete had even avoided marijuana during high school.

When his brother Bill left for college, things went badly for Josh. He became addicted to prescription painkillers. The problem with those, however, was that getting them illegally cost a lot. Josh, like many others, switched to heroin to chase the same feeling, but with a much cheaper price tag.

Heroin typically comes in powdered form, either brown, white, or some combination of the two. Many people who use heroin first became addicted to opiods by taking prescription painkillers.

Later, items went missing from their parents' house. These were the things Josh stole to pay for his growing habit. Trips home for Bill sometimes meant visiting local hotels and other scary places to find Josh on weekends. In the end, his family convinced him to go to rehab. Josh has been fighting his addiction since 2012.

Many victims get into heroin because they want to try something fun, even dangerous. Whatever the case, using heroin often leads to heroin abuse. Crawling out of an even short-term heroin addiction can be traumatic and difficult.

Heroin and similar hard drugs have often been misunderstood. So have addicts. To solve a problem, or cure an illness or condition, you must first diagnose it correctly. Myths surrounding the use of heroin, along with other, similar drugs that resemble heroin in their effects—known as opioids—are common. These myths have often worked to mislead even experts, much less laymen. This work can serve as part of a larger set of resources for readers to learn more about the tragic and ongoing public health disaster that heroin has brought. Armed with knowledge, they can work to prevent and fix the damage heroin has done to their towns, schools, and even families.

CHAPTER ONE

The Big H

Heroin is a big part of a larger and terrible problem: the opioid epidemic. Opioids are a kind of drug that affect the human body in similar ways. Opioids get their name from opium, a drug made from the poppy plant. Poppies grow in South America and Mexico and in Asian countries like Laos, Turkey, Afghanistan, and others.

The drugs made from the poppy are known as opiates. There are also man-made drugs that act like opiates. All of these fall under one category: opioids.

The poppy plant is grown all over the world, including Central Asia and Mexico, where criminal networks turn those poppy plants into narcotics.

As the Center on Addiction points out, "while all opiates are [considered] opioids, not all opioids are opiates." All opioids, the center adds, "[bind] to the brain's opioid receptors—the parts of the brain responsible for controlling pain, reward, and addictive behaviors."

Some well-known opiates are heroin, morphine, and codeine. Morphine and heroin were both used as medicines and painkillers throughout history. They were used for surgery long before modern anesthesia was invented. Anesthesia is any substance that can be put into the human body to lessen or kill pain.

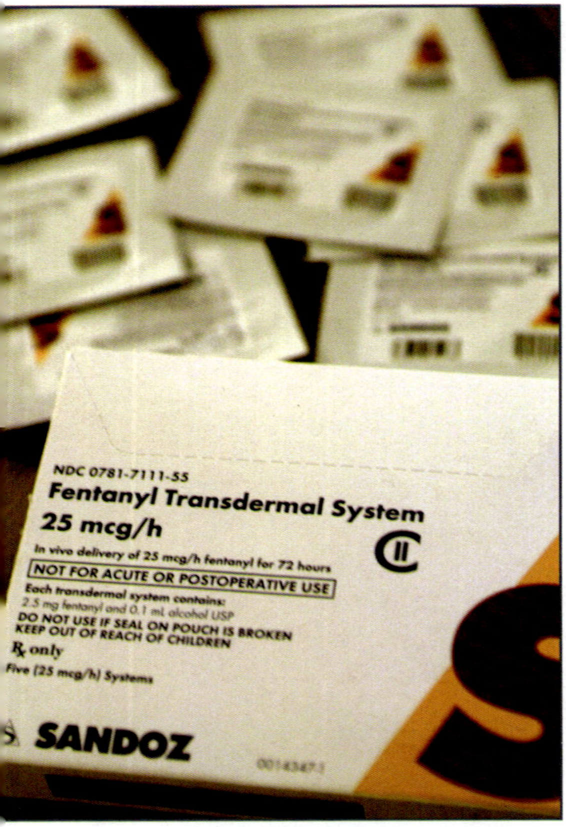

Many synthetic opioids were invented only recently. Others have been used on and off for decades. Fentanyl, for example, was invented in 1959. It is dozens of times more powerful than morphine. For years, it was only used in surgery and for limited special cases, like helping cancer sufferers reduce pain. In the 1990s, fentanyl patches came on the market. These were now available through doctors' offices, wearable at home and outside.

Fentanyl and other synthetic opioids cause the most overdose deaths in the United States. In 2016, nearly twenty thousand deaths were linked to the use of synthetic opioids.

HEROIN AND HISTORY

Heroin, opium, and other opioids have been used as medicine for thousands of years. The poppy plant was first grown in Lower Mesopotamia, part of southern Iraq. People later grew it all over the Mediterranean, including the Greeks, Romans, and many others. The Macedonian military conqueror Alexander the Great even introduced the plant to India and other places his forces entered in Asia.

In the nineteenth century, opium addiction exploded in China. China's government even tried to stop and control the drug's sale. But the opium trade was partly run by the British. The British imported opium from India. They even invaded China in the First Opium War (1839–1842) to make sure the trade would continue.

Friedrich Sertürner, a German, first isolated, or separated, morphine from the opium poppy in 1803. Morphine is about ten times as strong as opium. Its first wide use was as a painkiller during surgery for US Civil War troops. Hundreds of thousands of soldiers got hooked on morphine.

In 1874, scientists were trying to make another drug like morphine. One of them, Charles Romley Alder Wright, accidentally made what we now call heroin. Around the same time, a large German drug company named Bayer, which still operates today, was also working to produce a drug similar to morphine. The drug they wanted to make was called codeine. But the drug they ended up making was as much as twice as powerful as morphine itself. Bayer had made their own heroin, it turned out.

(continued on the next page)

(continued from the previous page)

In 1898, Bayer put the heroin they had created on the market. They sold it as a pain reliever. It was also supposed to be nonaddictive. People used it like some people use alcohol today. Bayer even sold it as a cure for children's colds. The word *heroisch* is German for "powerful." Bayer based the name "heroin" on it. Heroin was also the drug's early brand name. Its scientific name was diamorphine.

A Crisis of Addiction

Heroin and opium became such problems in the United States that lawmakers felt forced to act. Many communities even suffered mistreatment from governments and law enforcement agents because of it. Many Chinese people, for example, had moved to the United States in the middle to late nineteenth century. Opium dens, blamed on the Chinese, were thought of as places full of crime and other problems. Government officials and others used these as an excuse to spread hatred of the Chinese and pass laws against them

President Teddy Roosevelt, shown here in 1906, was concerned that America's drug problem was harming the country. He appointed a doctor, Hamilton Wright, as the country's first opium commissioner.

in California and other places. As for the drug itself, President Theodore Roosevelt even appointed an opium commissioner in 1908 to lead efforts to fight the problem.

The Harrison Narcotics Tax Act of 1914 was the first federal law to control opiates and other drugs. The Anti-Heroin Act of 1924 followed. Heroin has been considered a "hard drug" ever since. It is dangerous and addictive. People caught for crimes having to do with heroin usually get stiffer punishments.

Who Uses Heroin?

In the early twentieth century, desperate addicts were often seen looking for scrap metal or other junk to sell. They hoped to earn money for heroin. This activity earned them the nickname "junkies." Many addicts may do bad things to get money for their drugs. However, we must all remember that they are human beings who are suffering. Our first thought should be to help and heal such people, not harm and punish. That is because anyone you know can become an addict. A student-athlete can have major surgery and become addicted to opiates. The same can happen to a grandmother who falls and breaks her hip. Heroin can ruin anyone's life.

CHAPTER TWO

Your Mind and Body on Heroin

How does heroin affect the mind and body? It was once a mystery. Even now, it is still not fully understood. Lately, many people have grown desperate for answers. That is because the problem of heroin addiction has returned. It even seems bigger than ever.

Heroin can be taken in several ways. Users can swallow, smoke, snort, or inhale it. They can also inject it using a syringe. Long-term users like injecting the drug better. Injecting heroin gives the longest-lasting and most powerful high. Beginners may snort or smoke it before moving to needles. Some users may avoid needles. They hope to avoid diseases one can catch from sharing needles with others. Other people are simply afraid of the pain or are disgusted by the idea of needles generally.

What Heroin Does to the Body

Smoking, snorting, or injecting heroin sends it right to a person's brain. When it enters the human body, heroin changes how a person feels pleasure and pain. It also helps release chemicals called endorphins. Endorphins are responsible for controlling our feelings of happiness and well-being. The places they attach to in the brain are called opioid receptors.

When a person takes heroin, he will feel less pain. He will experience a slowdown in breathing and feel calmer. People who use heroin often feel a serious high, a burst of happiness and

A great achievement at school or on the athletic field can release feel-good chemicals called endorphins. Heroin can cause a similar high, but as time goes on users need more of the drug to reach that high.

well-being. Some people call this euphoria. When we normally feel happiness (without drugs), it is our own endorphins binding to these opioid receptor sites.

The brain and body of a healthy person has certain levels of endorphins. Heroin hits the brain at much higher levels than normal endorphins do. These high levels are partly what helps cause that intense, euphoric feeling. It is sometimes referred to as a heroin rush.

Normal events that might bring someone euphoric feelings might include winning a trophy in a school athletic event. Or imagine the feeling of finding out you got into your top college pick. Even having something really tasty to eat that you didn't expect can trigger an endorphin rush. So can hearing a favorite song.

The body can get confused by heroin and other drugs that have similar effects, however. With more opioids, a person's brain will grow more receptor sites. The body ends up needing more endorphins—or heroin or other opioids—to keep up with them. This creates the need or craving that heroin and other drugs are known for. Soon, the user will do anything to get them. The pain of being without an addictive substance is known as withdrawal. Withdrawal affects both the brain and body.

Heroin addiction happens differently for different people. Some become addicted after recovering from an injury or dealing with pain. Others run into friends at parties. A friend offers them the drug, and they think "why not?" Others might seek it out themselves because they are curious. No one who takes heroin plans to become addicted, even if they know its dangers.

THE DANGERS OF NEEDLES

Shooting heroin puts a person at risk for developing various diseases. Many heroin users do the drug with others. This sometimes includes using the same needles when shooting up. One heroin user can infect others with certain diseases. Addicts can catch a disease like hepatitis C, which affects the liver. A warning sign of hepatitis C and other kinds of hepatitis is when a user's eyes turn a yellowish color.

Users can also catch the human immunodeficiency virus, or HIV. HIV is the virus that causes acquired immunodeficiency syndrome (AIDS). HIV stops the human body from defending

(continued on the next page)

A health professional can answer any questions you may have about drug addiction and recovery. Everything you talk about must be kept confidential, so don't hesitate to express your concerns.

(continued from the previous page)

itself against sickness. If untreated, AIDS can lead to major problems—and can even kill the victim. It is bad enough when someone is dealing with drug addiction. No one needs to add a major illness to what is already a tough existence.

What Does It Feel Like?

The euphoria, or rush, of heroin is what many users first feel. Some people describe it as feeling calm, warm, safe, and completely worry free. Physically, heroin can affect users in different ways. Still, some effects are felt by most or all users. The body slows down. Everything moves slower, even the heart. Heroin users can feel distant or separated from their bodies or environments. Others might notice that they slur their speech. They can also be sleepy and distracted. Users can go between being awake and in a dreamlike, drugged-out state known as going "on the nod."

A first-time user often suffers from nausea. The drug convinces the brain that it needs to get rid of the heroin. The easiest way the brain knows how to do that is by triggering vomiting. The person might get headaches and feel other symptoms, too. This nausea might happen the first few times. This turns off some people enough that they end up avoiding heroin—the best decision.

The human reflex to cough is also affected by heroin. Taking a lot the first time and then risking vomiting while asleep is a recipe for disaster. People who are nodding off or simply asleep

Nausea is a common reaction to taking heroin for the first time. Hopefully, this negative experience is enough to keep teens from trying the drug a second time.

can easily choke on their own vomit. They will not even realize it is happening.

Taking a Big Risk

Not many people start using heroin by shooting it. Too many people are afraid of needles and heroin's bad reputation. As someone grows addicted, needles start to look appealing. Users know shooting dope will get them higher quicker.

To smoke heroin, users will dissolve the powdered form of the drug in a spoon with water. They heat that mixture up. They will then inhale the fumes rising from the heated mixture.

Snorting any powder is a very risky thing to do. With illegal drugs, you have no idea whether you are getting the drug you paid for or not.

Heroin used to be less pure and delivered a weaker high. Now there are more powerful "brands" of the drug. These brands of heroin can deliver a powerful high just by smoking them. People who smoke heroin risk damage to their lungs, throat, mouth, and lips.

Snorting is another way of taking heroin. With the drug in powder form, users might cut lines using a razor or plastic card like a credit card and snort the lines up into their nose using a straw or rolled-up piece of paper.

Like cocaine and other powdered drugs, snorting heroin often will damage your nose. This causes nosebleeds and breathing problems. It can also cause congestion. Meanwhile, Asthma sufferers and others who suffer lung and breathing problems are at especially high risk to make those problems worse by snorting the drug.

No Going Back

Someone can be an addict and never shoot heroin. But it is far more common for hardcore users to shoot the drug. Many people do so for years, even decades. When users want to shoot heroin, they begin by mixing the powder or other form of heroin. Brown and white are two forms of powder heroin easily mixed with water. Meanwhile, black tar heroin looks sticky and black. It can also be dissolved in water. The solutions are injected by users.

Addicts can quickly damage the veins in their arms and other parts of the body. It also gets worse as someone uses heroin over time. Repeated injections collapse blood vessels. The user needs to constantly find new vessels to use.

Long-term users of syringes can experience bad health problems. Collapsed vessels can get infected. Shooting also leaves scars called track marks. Shooting can cause bruising and users can even develop puffy hand syndrome, where the back of the hands become swollen. This may occur from quinine, an ingredient in some forms of heroin.

Many different diseases are spread by needle use. Some are curable, but others can be fatal. This is especially true for sicknesses that are untreated. The problem is that heroin is the most important thing to users. While they are addicted, their health comes second.

Heroin can harm different parts of the body. It leaves a dry and sticky feeling in the user's mouth. Her skin might get pale, cool, and clammy. Another problem is constipation—the inability to pass solid waste. Heroin users might also experience itchiness, rashes, and other skin conditions. Miosis occurs in the eyes when someone is high. Miosis means that a user's pupils get smaller, or constrict.

Another side effect of heroin is loss of appetite. Rapid weight loss is always a warning sign that a person is not doing well. Heroin addicts can even experience malnutrition. This means not having enough vitamins and minerals to grow and function. People always seeking a high often make feeding themselves a lower priority.

Overdose: Game Over

The greatest threat to the health and safety of heroin users is that of overdose. Overdose is such a great danger because heroin slows down the heart and other organs. The primary causes of death during an overdose are heart and respiratory failure.

Many addicts think they know exactly how much heroin they can take safely. But other situations make that tricky. For example, a new connection or friend might start getting the user a whole new brand of heroin. It might be much more powerful, or cut—or mixed—with other drugs or substances that harm, or even kill, the user. You simply never know for sure what something is mixed with.

Some users are more likely to suffer an overdose—and even die—if they have taken a break from the drug or if their supply stopped. Maybe they were in the hospital or even in jail. That is a dangerous situation to be in because one's tolerance may have dropped since last taking heroin.

CHAPTER THREE

Getting Hooked

Heroin creeps up on users. They may think they have things under control. Perhaps they only use the drug every other day. Then it becomes a daily habit. Soon, they are not just using after everyone else has gone to bed or out on the town. Instead, the user is finding excuses to do heroin right after school or work. It is not long before the same person is sneaking out of class for a bump or even to shoot up. By the time people have moved on to needles, it is possible they have already abandoned school, work, hobbies, and other things they used to enjoy.

Users build a dependence on the drug. This means their bodies physically need heroin. The more heroin people take, the fewer endorphins their bodies produce. This means that they constantly need to up their intake. Getting that euphoric high is the least of their worries now. They may still experience a rush or thrill occasionally but have to do a lot more of the drug to reach it. Few stay at the same heroin dose for long. Over time, they find it very hard to feel joy or pleasure without it.

A Downward Spiral

It is tough to watch someone get addicted to heroin. The signs may be hard to notice at first. Soon enough, friends and family begin to put two and two together. That is because heroin dramatically changes the life of anyone who does it. Heroin is both illegal and one of the most feared narcotics. Young people will likely hide their addiction for as long as possible.

The signs may begin with missing morning classes or leaving school early. Someone might end up missing lots of school or dropping out altogether. Because the heroin lifestyle requires dishonesty, that becomes a part of life for users and addicts. They must lie because telling the truth would expose them to punishment, including being forced to go to rehab. Any potential situation that might cut off the person's heroin supply must be avoided.

Young people can find themselves in a no-win situation. The same people that could help are the ones they are hiding their biggest secret from. In addition,

Some people turn to heroin because they feel depressed or disconnected from the world. But heroin addiction has a far more destructive effect on a person's mood.

shame and fear will stop many from getting help. No one wants to get in trouble. But a heroin addiction is enough of a problem that no one can keep it a secret for very long. The user goes through changes in his appearance, personality, and habits that few people can ignore over the long term.

Parents, friends, and other trusted adults, like teachers and coaches, may not notice at first. But it is hard to deny something is wrong when a teen skips school or football practice or hides in his room when he's home. His loved ones will be so concerned that they may stage an intervention, a meeting where they tell the addict that he is sick and needs help.

HEROIN AND CRIME

No one enters a life of addiction and crime because he is a bad person. All kinds of people become heroin abusers. Even people who end up robbing people or committing other crimes to support their habit are not bad people. They are sick and need help.

One problem is that heroin users think they can continue to function normally on heroin. Most people cannot. Young people, especially, will probably not have the money to support their habit. To make up the shortfall, they will at first use whatever resources they can. Then they will borrow from whomever they can. It becomes nearly impossible for hardcore users to hold a job.

Once their money runs out, they must get more. At first, they may sell their things. The user might commit petty crimes. Some people steal bags, phones, and other things from public places

(continued on the next page)

(continued from the previous page)

or even friends' homes. They will steal jewelry, electronics, and other valuables, as well as money, from any friend or family member they can. Often, the simplest plan is to start selling heroin themselves. Dealing the drug gives them money and easier access to a supply. This opens them up to more risk. They must fear the police, other criminals, and other addicts.

Heroin use can be very hard on the user's family, too. Sometimes they must make the tough choice to force them to go to rehab or even report them to law enforcement if their behavior becomes threatening or violent.

Shoplifting is just one crime addicts engage in to feed their heroin habit. They may move on to more serious crimes that can have a devastating effect on their lives and relationships.

Withdrawal Worries

Addicts who stop doing heroin will experience withdrawal. Depending on the person, it can start anywhere from six to twelve hours after the last dose or use. Withdrawal can last as long as a week or more. Most users say that two or three days into withdrawal is the most painful period. Some people experience withdrawal symptoms for weeks. Others even suffer for months. It is a delicate and crucial time. Depressed users might experience suicidal thoughts. Six hours without heroin is one thing. It can turn into a full-blown panic attack when the addict cannot get a fix by twelve hours or longer.

After some time, the user is anticipating the next high. The body is beginning to crave heroin. Meanwhile, the happiness and euphoria of heroin use is gone. Awful feelings come rushing in. These can include bad memories that many users find tough to handle. Over time, some people are at risk for even bigger psychological problems, such as psychosis. They might have a breakdown and have to go to the hospital. Someone who is feeling this unhappy needs medical care quickly.

Drug withdrawal is one of the most horrific experiences a person can go through. The person's body is craving heroin, but the high she used to enjoy is gone, which can lead to mental heath issues.

As time goes by, heroin leaves the user's system. He becomes far more sensitive to physical pain. Withdrawal from heroin might cause joint, bone, and muscle pain and discomfort. Stomach cramps, muscle spasms, lower back pain, headaches, and other painful symptoms are also common.

Think of the worst flu you have ever experienced. Now imagine it a good deal worse, with nausea, vomiting, diarrhea, and fever. A body in withdrawal will also overproduce fluids, like mucus, tears, and sweat. It is all part of the body fighting its way back to health.

Hitting Rock Bottom

Heroin ruins lives, including of those who try to kick it for years but never quite succeed. If people are lucky, their addiction might last only a few months. Teens or college students whose parents discover their habit probably have a better chance to recover since they have a fighting chance if they tackle the problem early.

At every step, there are concrete decisions people can make to declare that they won't be foolish enough to risk their health and safety for a bit of passing pleasure. It gets harder as the weeks, months, and even years go by to even think about quitting.

After all, the life of a hardcore heroin user is sad, scary, and dangerous. Addicts often find shelter at the homes of other addicts, or they squat in abandoned buildings or homeless encampments. Often, their own families have kicked them out or they have run away from them.

In addition, the daily routine of addicts is also frustrating and uncertain. From the minute they wake up, they must figure out a way they will obtain money to get the fix they need for that

DOS AND DON'TS

Do visit trusted government, counseling, recovery, and medical information sites to get the best and most current information about heroin.
Don't trust everything you read in the darkest corners of the internet. When it comes to heroin and drugs in general, there are many inaccurate and misleading sites out there.

Do ask your school counselors, teachers, and other trusted adults about heroin and other drugs.
Don't rely on secondhand or suspicious information from friends or others who might not have the full story.

Do keep an eye out for friends and acquaintances who may be acting strangely or seem "off" or not themselves. Ask about their well-being and offer to be someone to talk to if they need help or advice.
Don't expose, dox, or otherwise reveal someone else's drug problem to others, whether to friends, family, law enforcement, or other authority figures. An exception should be made in the case of a real emergency, but it is best to let others make their own decisions.

day and night. Every day is a struggle to get that money and hopefully some for food and other needs. Many addicts suffer from depression, which may have contributed to their drug problem in the first place.

CHAPTER FOUR

The Road to Recovery

Many addicts think about quitting all the time. Sometimes they have to hit rock bottom to make that important decision. Addicts realize that they need to escape their situation, or they will probably die. It might take a friend or family member overdosing—or some other traumatic event—for the addict to get to the point of wanting help.

First Steps

Once addicts have made up their minds to quit taking heroin, the first step is to detox, or detoxify, from the drug and any other substances. Detoxification means cleaning one's body of heroin and its effects. There is no easy way to do this. Some users think they can gradually withdraw. This means using less and less heroin slowly over time. Few users are able to quit successfully this way, as it takes an incredible amount of willpower and discipline.

A teen reads in her room at Tracey's Place of Hope, a drug and alcohol recovery center in Loomis, California. It's important for teens to explore the pros and cons of every rehabilitation center to find the best fit.

The same thing can be said about going cold turkey. Cold turkey means quitting without taking any other treatments or medications to help with withdrawal. Users are in for a very hard road if they choose this way of detoxing. The addict can also relapse anytime. Relapse occurs when someone starts taking heroin again.

Addicts can check themselves into a rehabilitation, or rehab, facility. Often, they are admitted by another person, like a parent or someone else in charge of their care. Addicts' families might have to pay to get their child into a recovery program if the program is not covered by insurance. There are rehab facilities run by local, state, and federal government agencies. Some people might stay in a rehab center for just a few days, while others are there for a year or longer. It all depends on how severe the patient's problem is.

A Little Assist

Most medical professionals advise against going cold turkey as a way of quitting heroin. They strongly suggest using drugs that fight withdrawal symptoms and help addicts in other ways.

There are drugs that satisfy addicts' cravings for heroin, but with fewer side effects. Methadone is one example of this kind

HOPE ON WHEELS AGAINST HEROIN

One big problem for many heroin and other opioid addicts is getting the resources they need. Many live in rural areas, far from cities and towns. Addiction treatment can be tough to find, much less get to. Some recovery professionals have taken things into their own hands.

One example that CNN reported on in March 2019 is Pennsylvania's Positive Recovery Solutions. The organization has attached a recreational vehicle (RV) to a pickup truck to create a moving opioid addiction clinic. Every day, logistics coordinator Stuart Masula loads up to drive around and help addicts all over rural Pennsylvania. Masula delivers a form of naltrexone called Vivitrol to users. This form of the drug has an extended release. It helps addicts control their heroin or

(continued on next page)

(continued from the previous page)

other opioid cravings so they can get through the day without buying drugs.

The mobile clinic's team also offers counseling. It is all the brainchild of chief operating officer (COO) and registered nurse Amanda Cope. Cope told CNN she started sneaking alcohol at age nine and was a full-blown alcoholic by age sixteen. The RV clinic takes new and returning patients. It is just one team on the frontlines of the war against heroin and opioid addiction.

Recovery services are so hard to find in some parts of the country that heroin addicts have to rely on mobile counseling centers like the one shown here.

of drug. It is also an opioid, and it is part of many rehab and substance abuse programs. Addicts all over the country go to special clinics where they get a daily dose of methadone as part of recovery programs. The dose is not supposed to get users high. Instead, it removes the urge to do heroin itself. This helps them continue on with their day.

Methadone has its own issues. Some addicts try to avoid it and other opioids. They see methadone treatment as just trading one dependence for another. Methadone also has its own withdrawal symptoms. They include many of the same discomforts of heroin withdrawal. Some patients are allergic to methadone. Taking it would harm or even kill them.

Alternatives to methadone work in similar ways. Another drug is buprenorphine, sold under the brand name Subutex. According to Drugabuse.gov, "Buprenorphine relieves drug cravings without producing the 'high' or dangerous side effects of other opioids." One brand of the drug, Suboxone, is even designed to force withdrawal symptoms if someone still suffering from heroin addiction tries to inject it instead of taking it by mouth, as it is prescribed. The Food and Drug Administration (FDA) also approved the drug to be prescribed by doctors. For a long time, only special treatment clinics could give out drugs like methadone. Yet another drug used in heroin recovery is naltrexone, which blocks other opioids from working in the body. Patients can't get high off them while taking it. It has had mixed results, however. Forms of naltrexone that only have to be administered once a month—instead of daily methadone or other drugs—may make the drug more popular over time.

People going through recovery need to know their options. They should have the best information to make the best decision for them. Remember: methadone and other drugs aren't magic bullets that will cure or eliminate heroin addiction. It is up to each person to use all the tools necessary not to relapse.

RELIABLE RESOURCES

There are many established organizations that specialize in fighting drug addiction. They can help both addicts and those who love them. Here are several places to go for information and assistance:

- **Narcotics Anonymous** (https://www.na.org): NA is the best-known recovery system. It is a twelve-step program founded in 1953. Its attendees agree to engage in twelve steps to help in their recovery from drugs. These steps include examining themselves, seeking forgiveness from those they have hurt, and other positive actions.
- **SMART Recovery** (https://www.smartrecovery.org): Short for Self-Management and Recovery Training, this four-part program focuses on building and maintaining motivation; coping with urges; managing thoughts, feelings, and behavior; and living a balanced life.
- **Substance Abuse and Mental Health Services Administration** (SAMHSA) (1-800-662-HELP): This federal agency offers those struggling with addiction information and referrals to local organizations that can assist them in their recovery.

Ins and Outs of Recovery

For many substance abusers, changing locations can be an important step. They recover more easily away from all the negative influences in their daily lives. That is why some recovery patients prefer inpatient rehab. Inpatient care means living on site at a facility. Tight schedules and structure provide users the support they need to recover. They are also away from drug-abusing friends and acquaintances.

Inpatient recovery also includes on-site resources. These include one-to-one therapy with mental health professionals. Patients might also do group work, in which recovering addicts sit and talk about their sobriety, their traumas, and derive support

One major component of addiction recovery is dealing with issues that are holding you back. Some teens feel more comfortable speaking in a support group, while others prefer private therapy sessions.

from one another. Some addicts like being far from negative influences or even from toxic family members, partners, or friends involved in their addictive behavior.

Still, inpatient care is not for everyone. It is hard for people without much money or spare time to go to rehab. If they work full-time, it may be impossible to stay at a treatment facility for a month or more. Nearby outpatient care may be a better choice for them. They can get the treatment they need and be home at the end of the day. They might also prefer staying close to home. For some people, being far away from loved ones makes it more difficult to recover.

The Long Way Home

Addiction and its painful memories can't be erased. However, every day millions of people wake up having gone through heroin dependence and addiction, and they start their days ready to stay sober—one day at a time. Of course, some addicts never get better. Many die or continue to live with their addictions for years on end.

One important thing for recovering heroin users to remember is that there is light at the end of the tunnel, even though recovery is never easy. No one is ever truly cured from addiction, and heroin is one of the toughest of all drugs to kick in the first place—and to stay away from in the long term.

Recovery from heroin abuse takes a lot of time and effort. Some people refer to it as putting in the work. Obviously, the best decision is to never get involved with heroin to begin with. As a person recovers, they start to reconnect with people. These may be family members they have stolen from or otherwise hurt.

Martial arts, like the karate demonstrated by this teen, can be helpful for recovering addicts because it instills discipline, drive, and a sense of greater purpose.

It could be former employers they have disappointed or friends they have betrayed. Much of the time, these are exactly the people the addict needs in their life. Few people recover or stay clean without some kind of support.

One long-term strategy for recovering addicts is to find things that they like to do outside of the drug scene. Many people exercise, taking part in yoga, martial arts, or working out at the gym. They find that physical activity makes them happy and gives them the discipline they need to stay clean. Someone in recovery can get involved in music by taking lessons or even starting a band. Painting, collecting stamps or other collectibles, going to the movies, and many other activities can take the place of the cycle of addiction.

Others find that taking care of underlying mental illnesses and conditions can go a long way to preventing a relapse. Whatever road they take, heroin addicts need the help of friends and family. Be there for someone if they need your support. Having someone to turn to in times of crisis can make all the difference. They'll learn they can count on you, and you'll be reminded of just how dangerous using drugs can be.

GLOSSARY

COLD TURKEY The process of quitting an addictive substance—like heroin or alcohol—suddenly, with little or no assistance from medication or treatment, often causing painful withdrawal symptoms.

CUTTING The process of mixing drugs with other substances to make a dealer more profits.

ENDORPHINS Chemicals within the human body and brain that help manage pleasure, pain, and happiness.

FENTANYL A potent opioid painkiller used as pain medication and sometimes in surgical anesthesia.

HEPATITIS An inflammation of the liver, often caused by the hepatitis virus, one risk of using and sharing infected needles.

HUMAN IMMUNODEFICIENCY VIRUS (HIV) A potentially fatal virus that attacks the body's immune system, HIV causes the disease known as acquired immunodeficiency syndrome (AIDS).

INPATIENT Referring to care received during an extended stay in a hospital, rehab, or other care facility.

JUNKIE A mean-spirited slang term for a heroin addict. Its use should be discouraged but may still be encountered in many situations.

MORPHINE An opiate derived directly from the poppy plant, long used for treating pain.

NODDING OFF A symptom of heroin use in which the user goes into and out of a dreamlike state while high.

OPIATE Any drug derived naturally from the poppy plant with properties similar to heroin.

OPIOID Any natural or synthetic drug with similar properties to heroin.

OUTPATIENT Refers to treatment received for drug addiction or other ailments that requires daily or semidaily contact with medical professionals and no overnight or extended stay in a care facility.

OXYCODONE One of several synthetic opiates used to treat severe pain.

REHAB Short for "rehabilitation," this refers to any program in which people recover from their addiction.

RELAPSE When people fail to stay sober and instead go back to using the substance they are addicted to.

SYRINGE A tiny pump and needle assembly that is used to inject something into the bloodstream or to draw blood, sometimes simply referred to as a needle.

TOLERANCE A person's ability to handle certain amounts of a drug or alcohol.

FOR MORE INFORMATION

Canadian Centre on Substance Use and Addiction (CCSA)
75 Albert Street, Suite 500
Ottawa, ON K1P 5E7
Canada
(833) 235-4048
Website: http://www.ccdus.ca
Twitter: @CCSACanada
YouTube: @CCSA.CCDUS
The CCSA combats substance abuse among Canadians. It works with various public and private organizations to craft programs and awareness campaigns.

Canadian Institute for Substance Use Research (CISUR)
University of Victoria
Technology Enterprise Facility
Victoria, BC V8P 5C2
Canada
(250) 472-5445
Email: cisur@uvic.ca
Website: https://www.uvic.ca/research/centres/cisur
Twitter: @UVic_CISUR
The CISUR, formerly the Centre for Addictions Research of BC, brings together groups and individuals to study substance use and addiction and to lead community-wide efforts at harm reduction.

Narcotics Anonymous
PO Box 9999
Van Nuys, CA 91409
(818) 773-9999
Website: https://www.na.org
Narcotics Anonymous, commonly known as NA, is the largest international twelve-step program, serving as a supportive community for those recovering from drug addiction.

National Association of Addiction Treatment Providers (NAATP)
The Chancery Building
1120 Lincoln Street, Suite 1104
Denver, CO 80203
(888) 574-1008
Email: info@naatp.org
Website: https://www.naatp.org
Instagram: @naatpofficial
Twitter: @naatpoffice
The NAATP is an association of various substance abuse treatment programs and providers nationwide that offers leadership, advocacy, and support services to its members.

National Institute on Drug Abuse (NIDA)
6001 Executive Boulevard, Room 5213, MSC 9561
Bethesda, MD 20892
(301) 443-1124
Website: https://www.drugabuse.gov
Facebook: @NIDANIH
Twitter: @NIDAnews

Part of the National Institutes of Health (NIH), NIDA is one of the largest institutions in the United States to research addiction, drug use, and treatment.

Smart Recovery Canada
223 12th Avenue SW
Calgary, AB T2R 0G9
Canada
(403) 619-4210
Website: http://smartrecovery.ca
Smart Recovery runs free self-help programs for substance abusers to recover in nurturing environments. Volunteers assist addicts in changing self-defeating thinking, emotions, and actions.

FOR FURTHER READING

Abramowitz, Melissa, and Andrew C. Harris. *Heroin and Prescription Opioids*. Minneapolis, MN: Essential Library/ ABDO Publishing, 2019.

Allen, John. *The Dangers of Heroin*. San Diego, CA: ReferencePoint Press, 2017.

Bryan, Bethany. *Heroin, Opioid, and Painkiller Abuse*. New York, NY: Rosen Publishing, 2019.

Cashin, John. *The Heroin Crisis*. Philadelphia, PA: Mason Crest Publishers, 2018.

Hamen, Susan E. *Heroin and Its Dangers*. San Diego, CA: ReferencePoint Press, 2020.

Horning, Nicole. *Heroin: Killer Drug Epidemic*. New York, NY: Lucent Press, 2017.

Marsico, Katie. *Heroin*. New York, NY: Cavendish Square, 2014.

Parks, Peggy J. *Heroin Addiction*. San Diego, CA: ReferencePoint Press, 2015.

Perritano, John. *Opioids: Heroin, Oxycontin, and Painkillers*. Broomall, PA: Mason Crest Publishers, 2016.

Uhl, Xina M. *Who Is Using Opioids and Opiates?* Broomall, PA: Mason Crest Publishers, 2018.

BIBLIOGRAPHY

Booth, Martin. *Opium: A History*. New York, NY: Simon & Schuster, 1996.

Freedman, Hannah. "We Asked, You Answered: Is There a Difference Between an Opioid and an Opiate?" Center on Addiction, September 28, 2017. https://www.centeronaddiction.org/the-buzz-blog/we-asked-you-answered-there-difference-between-opioid-and-opiate.

Holmes, Kristen, and Katelyn Petroka. "Mobile Addiction Clinic Brings Help to Those at Heart of Opioid Epidemic." CNN, March 8, 2019. https://www.cnn.com/2019/03/08/health/mobile-addiction-treatment-clinic/index.html.

Izaguirre, Anthony. "In a City Ravaged by Heroin, a Needle Exchange Stalls." *Seattle Times*, October 31, 2017. https://www.seattletimes.com/nation-world/in-a-city-ravaged-by-heroin-a-needle-exchange-stalls.

National Institute on Drug Abuse. "What Are the Treatments for Heroin Use Disorder?" Retrieved March 1, 2019. https://www.drugabuse.gov/publications/research-reports/heroin/what-are-treatments-heroin-use-disorder.

Public Broadcasting System (PBS). "The Opium Kings." 1998. Retrieved February 17, 2019. https://www.pbs.org/wgbh/pages/frontline/shows/heroin/etc/history.html.

Pyhtila, Jessica. "Understanding What Heroin Does to the Brain." The Recovery Village, February 15, 2019. https://www.therecoveryvillage.com/heroin-addiction/understanding-heroin-brain/#gref.

Robson, Philip. *Forbidden Drugs*. Oxford, United Kingdom: Oxford University Press, 2002.

Sotonoff, Jamie. "Suburban Heroin Problem Called 'A Medical Emergency." *Chicago Daily Herald,* March 11, 2013. https://www.dailyherald.com/article/20130311/news/703119782.

Stein, Rob. "Life Expectancy Drops as Opioid Deaths Surge." Shots: Health News from NPR, December 21, 2017. https://www.npr.org/sections/health-shots/2017/12/21/572080314/life-expectancy-drops-again-as-opioid-deaths-surge-in-u-s.

Trethan, Phaedra. "Families Share Stories Behind Camden County's Opioid Lawsuit." *Courier-Post,* February 24, 2018. https://www.courierpostonline.com/story/news/2018/02/23/camden-county-opioid-lawsuit-personal-stories/354450002.

INDEX

About the Author

Philip Wolny is a writer and editor living in New York City. He was born in Poland and grew up in Queens. He has written numerous books for adolescent readers. His works span topics such as self-help, addiction and recovery, health and wellness, teen sports, career planning, and online safety. His titles for Rosen include *The Truth About Heroin*, *Defeating Gangs in Your Neighborhood and Online*, and *Chemical Reactions*.

Photo Credits

Cover Evdokimov Maxim/Shutterstock.com; p. 5 H.S. Photos/Alamy Stock Photo; p. 7 allou/Shutterstock.com; p. 8 Glenn Koenig/Los Angeles Times/Getty Images; p. 10 Library of Congress Prints and Photographs; p. 13 fizkes/Shutterstock.com; p. 15 Alexander Raths/Shutterstock.com; p. 17 VGstockstudio/Shutterstock.com; p. 18 tugol/Shutterstock.com; p. 22 LeoGrand/E+/Getty Images; p. 24 Matthias Tunger/Photodisc/Getty Images; p. 25 gawrav/E+/Getty Images; p. 29 Tribune Content Agency LLC/Alamy Stock Photo; p. 31 © AP Images; p. 34 ClarkandCompany/iStock/Getty Images; p. 36 Chris Stein/DigitalVision/Getty Images; back cover and interior speech bubbles sumkinn/Shutterstock.com.

Design and Layout: Nicole Russo-Duca; Editor: Jennifer Landau; Photo Researcher: Sherri Jackson